500+ AFFIRMATIONS TO DEVELOP MENTAL TOUGHNESS FOR ATHLETES & ENTREPRENEURS

POSITIVE SELF-TALK TO PERFORM UNDER PRESSURE

BRIAN O'GRADY
&
THOMAS PATRICK

SPECIAL BONUS

Want the Audiobook and this bonus book for Free?

Audiobook   **Bonus Ebook**

Join the community and get the Audiobook version + this Bonus Ebook for Free

SCAN CODE WITH YOUR PHONE CAMERA

Table of Contents

BRIAN O'GRADY & THOMAS PATRICK

INTRODUCTION

This is a book of affirmations and self-talk for peak athletic performance and developing unwavering mental toughness. Whether you play a team sport or an individual one, the content in this book will help you reach new levels. Replace the word 'game' with 'event' if it's not a team sport you play. It could be motor racing, athletics, or even chess. You could be a musician who dreams of playing in front of sold-out arenas. It does not matter. The characteristics and traits for reaching the top of any field are all the same. The material in this book can also be related to business and entrepreneurship. In progressing up the ladder of your chosen career, you will face similar adversities and setbacks that an athlete will face, and you will need to develop the same attributes to get through them. You will also have days when you must 'perform' at your best under pressure. These affirmations will help you do just that. You can navigate through this book how you please. If you want to jump straight to the affirmations, go right ahead. You can come back to whichever section resonates with you at any stage.

The word *'affirmations'* gets a bad rap these days, and sometimes rightly so. Thanks to social media, particularly Instagram and TikTok, you now have millions of people sitting at home saying to themselves, *'I'm rich, I'm rich,*

I'm rich, I'm happy, I'm happy, I'm happy' hundreds of times over while living from paycheck to paycheck barely making ends meet. While the idea is correct, the execution is entirely wrong. You cannot trick the subconscious mind that easily. Deep down inside, most people don't believe what they're saying with these affirmations. They may believe it for a period, but when their outside circumstances don't align with these words and something bad happens, they often crumble and fall back into old thinking habits. They say to themselves, *'This is a load of BS spiritual nonsense. I'm not wasting my time with this again.'*

What you really need to do is light a fire inside your soul. You need to prepare yourself for the fact that, yes, this is your current reality. It's not what you want, and it's not going to change anytime soon. There will be setbacks and testing times along the way where you question everything. Take it as the universe challenging you to see if you have the resolve to really make a change. If you can mentally prepare yourself for all the challenges that lay ahead, you will be in a far better position to see your affirmations come to life. So, what you really ought to say to yourself is, *'I accept my current circumstances. It's not where I want to be. I know there will be challenges ahead, but if I can persevere, clearly envision my future, and consistently say these affirmations and self-talk over and over and over, one of these days, I will begin to truly believe them. They will become a reality. My self-talk will overpower my subconscious mind.'*

Particularly during tough times, you need to override the program that has been running you for years. You need to feel now as though you already have what you want. You need to be consistent. Your dream and vision will become a reality if you do those things. This relates to athletes, businessmen, artists, and people from all other walks of life.

Once you are mentally prepared for the challenges your mind will face when using affirmations, it becomes a lot easier. You understand how it works. You understand that 99% of it is simply about OVERPOWERING the doubts with your self-talk. This is why I prefer the term self-talk. It's a weapon you learn to use. You are constantly in conversation with yourself. Your ego, as Eckhart Tolle refers to it, is constantly talking and often doubting you. It takes an enormous amount of awareness to realize that your ego is not you. You are the awareness behind your ego, the watcher.

So, you will notice that the affirmations in this book are much deeper than usual and a lot more intense. This is to stir up something deep inside you, a burning ambition, a fire that cannot be put out. Only by developing this fire and this spirit can you truly make a change and bring these affirmations to life. Of all the spiritual teachers out there on the topic of self-talk and manifestation, I suggest Neville Goddard be the main one you follow if you want to dive further into this.

SECTIONS EXPLAINED

SECTION 1 - UPCOMING GAME / EVENT

This book is broken into two main sections and a third separate bonus section. In section one, you have three immediate sets of affirmations you can use for an upcoming game or event. The first set of affirmations is to be used the day or night before a game. The next set can be used on the morning of a game. And the final set is reflection affirmations to use the evening or night AFTER a game or event. Most people do not reflect correctly after a game or performance. They do not debrief when things go well and what they did well in terms of preparation and mindset. Similarly, they don't reflect on things when they don't go so well and end up repeating the same mistakes in the future. You can come back to section 1 time and again whenever you feel necessary.

SECTION 2 – THE JOURNEY

Day 1 – Choose Your Hard
Day 2 – Comeback Season
Day 3 – Misunderstood

Day 4 – The Puma / Stealth Mode
Day 5 – Cementing Greatness
Day 6 – Demon Time / The Doubts
Day 7 – Inspiration from History
Day 8 - Spirit and Perseverance
Day 9 – Judgement Day
Day 10 – Reflecting Back

Section 2 is different from section 1. Section 2 takes you on a journey broken into 10 days, listed as DAY 1, DAY 2, DAY 3, and so on. The days metaphorically represent the journey a person or athlete goes through in a whole season or even in a whole career. It's a rollercoaster of emotions, of mental warfare, a war that is usually between yourself and your ego, your doubts. For example, DAY 1 could represent starting out on your journey in pre-season, and DAY 5 could be a few weeks or months later when you are flying high and performing well. DAY 6 can represent a difficult time period where you face doubts. So when that time does occur, you can read back over DAY 6 and deal with those doubts in real-time. DAY 10 represents the end of the season, reflecting back on what you personally achieved and learned along the way. And how you can potentially even improve further.

My advice is to sit back someday and read or listen to the full 10 days right the way through. That way, you will understand all the ups and downs you are about to face on this journey. The content of some days may resonate with you, while others may not. There is a mix of inspiration from history, learning from predatorial animals and how they perform under pressure, facing questions and doubts humans go through when rising to the top of any field, and learning to persevere and overcome those doubts. You will discover that the most liberating feeling of all is overcoming yourself. Once you have gone through it entirely, you can come back anytime to whatever day fits your current circumstances.

I believe these affirmations and self-talk have the power to help you develop a mental toughness and steeliness that will separate you from the rest. That will make you feel unstoppable, unbreakable. The number one attribute of top-performing athletes is how they handle adversity and keep going. 90% of the work is done just by showing up every day. Most people fall off on their dreams and ambitions as soon as they hit bumps along the way, be it in business or sporting careers.

So, you can interpret the journey however you like. You could be halfway through a season and want to turn things around. You could be just beginning a new career and want to make it to the top. You could be a young rookie just starting out, excited and ready to make waves in your sport or chosen field.

On the other hand, you could be an athlete coming to the end of their career who never quite reached their potential but is ready to put down a season like no other. There are so many examples of athletes who end up having their best season in their mid 30's, proving that in modern times, age is just a number. Karim Benzema, the French soccer player, just had the best season of his career in every aspect at 34 years of age. Lebron James is turning 38. His numbers have not dropped. In fact, he put in some of the highest stats of his career over the last few seasons. Nothing can stop you from pulling a season of your life out of the bag but you.

You could also be a middle-aged person with some extra pounds to shed who has rarely stepped inside a gym before and is not feeling the most energetic. 3 – 6 months of dedication to your fitness could turn your world upside down. Becoming fit and lean, having extra energy and a spring in your step, will feel amazing. It will also shock people close to you if you have never done anything like this before. It's never too late to start a worthwhile pursuit. You could be adding years to your life in that instance. Yes, some of the words in this book might not be directly related to that situation or someone climbing the ladder in the business world. But the words don't matter. It's the feelings that matter, the feelings generated inside that can ignite a flame for something special.

SECTION 3 –
BONUS INTERACTIVE RESOURCES

A – Finding Your Why
B – What's Blocking You
C – Visualization Exercises
D – The Habit Builder
E – Guided Box Breathing
F – Emotion-Stirring Music

This section is separate from the affirmations part of the book. You can read through this section before or after the affirmations. This section contains some interactive questions and exercises to discover or rediscover your *why*. Your *why* is why you play your chosen sport or hobby to begin with, what got you involved in it, and so forth. They are thought-provoking questions. The answers you provide will help cement in your mind why you do what you do and why it is a passion. There are also exercises to help you discover your true passion if you're still unsure. Once you clearly define your 'why, it becomes a lot easier to train hard, to keep going, and to push through difficult circumstances.

We will also identify '*What's Blocking You*' from achieving your dream and what circumstances or limiting beliefs are getting in the way. What excuses are you making?

Next, there are '*Visualization Exercises*' which can be extremely powerful when done correctly. After this is '*The Habit Builder,*' which explains what a habit is and how to slowly introduce healthy habits into your daily routine, bringing you closer to your dream or ambition. Many people have the wrong idea about building habits and how to do it. I will also show you how to simply track your habits and progress, keeping you accountable.

Finally, we have the music suggestions and the '*Guided Box Breathing*' resource, which you can go to whenever you feel anxious or stressed.

<u>SECTION 1 – UPCOMING GAME/EVENT</u>

The Day or Night Before the Game/Event

- ø The work is done.
- ø I know I've got this.
- ø I am strong and powerful.
- ø I am calm, knowing that I have prepared myself as best I can.
- ø The rest is in God's hands.
- ø I needn't stress or worry.
- ø Whatever happens, happens.
- ø I just know I will give it my all.
- ø I am quietly confident.
- ø While there may be nerves, there is also excitement.
- ø I cannot wait for the game to start to showcase my ability.
- ø I will have a stillness and determination about me.

- ø I will have laser focus and carry a deep look of determination in my eyes.
- ø The eyes don't lie. They are the gateway to the soul.
- ø And my eyes are crystal clear.
- ø Nothing can stop me.
- ø I will not waste any mental energy between now and game time worrying about different aspects of the game.
- ø If thoughts arise, I will let them come and go, not identifying with them, and giving them minimal attention.
- ø If I need to revise game plans or tactics, I will give myself time to do so.
- ø But like I said earlier, the work is done, so I will not worry regardless.
- ø Studies have proven that when muscles are calm and relaxed, they are at their most powerful.
- ø However, tension can and will arise from time to time, as is only natural.
- ø It's important not to resist it. Welcome it in.
- ø Any tension or stress I may feel, I will allow it to be there. I will sit with it, and I will let it go.
- ø By accepting any nervous tension that arises and letting it flow through me, it is released.
- ø If it comes, I will center myself.

- ø Next, we are going to take 4 deep boxed breaths. These breaths can be done at any time, whether there is tension or not.

***(A full guide on box breathing is included in Section 3 of this book)

- ø This calms the body and activates the parasympathetic nervous system
- ø It entails a 4-second slow inhale through the nose. Then a 4-second hold. Followed by a 4-second slow exhale through the mouth. And finally, a 4-second hold after the exhale.
- ø All we need to do is focus on our breathing.
- ø We are going to do it 3 times. That means in 1 full minute, you will have taken only 3 full breaths.
- ø Before we begin, breathe out fully and empty your lunges **take 3-4 seconds.

■■■

1. Now, let's inhale through the nose (slow count for 4 seconds).
2. Hold for 4 seconds (slow count for 4 seconds).
3. Release slowly through the mouth for 4 seconds (slow count for 4 seconds).
4. Hold for 4 seconds (slow count for 4 seconds).

5. Now we go again. Inhale through the nose (slow count for 4 seconds).
6. Hold for 4 seconds (slow count for 4 seconds).
7. Release slowly through the mouth (slow count for 4 seconds).
8. Hold for 4 seconds (slow count for 4 seconds).

9. And one last time, inhale through the nose (slow count for 4 seconds).
10. Hold for 4 seconds (slow count for 4 seconds).
11. Release slowly through the mouth (slow count for 4 seconds).
12. Hold for 4 seconds (slow count for 4 seconds).

Ø How does that feel?

Ø I am now centered and aligned with my true inner nature.

Ø There is a confidence and stillness deep inside me.

Ø I am calm. I am relaxed. I am READY.

Ø I AM.

Ø Win, lose or draw, I know I will give it my all with every last drop of blood, sweat, and tears.

Ø Representing this team, wearing this jersey. Playing with my teammates and friends means the world to me.

Ø I will do anything for them, as they would for me.

Ø Knowing this fills me with immense pride and passion.

Ø I am privileged to have this opportunity, and I don't take it for granted.

Ø I am going to enjoy this game and have fun.

Ø I know now that I have prepared myself as best I can, both mentally and physically.

Ø I know I am an outstanding athlete.

Ø I have total confidence in my ability.

- ø I will rest easy and go about my day and night as usual, not worried.
- ø If tension arises, I know what to do and how to release it.
- ø Similarly, before the game tomorrow, I will be at ease, loose, and nimble.
- ø Come game time; I will be ready to rock.
- ø I will return to this block of affirmations whenever I feel like it.

Gameday Morning

> Today is mine.
> Whether it's raining outside or the sun is shining, it does not matter.
> My competitors can worry about outside circumstances, not me.
> If I woke up feeling fresh after a great night's sleep, fantastic.
> If I had a poor night's sleep, tossing and turning, also fantastic.
> Navy seals can operate on minimal sleep for days.
> Our ancestors, likewise. Hunting for food and keeping out of danger just to survive.
> This is just a game at the end of the day.
> I think I'll survive an average night's sleep.
> There have been world champions who performed on their biggest days while being sleep-deprived, sick, or injured.
> Either way, it's all irrelevant.
> Today is already written. My faith is already sealed. It's in God's hands.

> But trust me, I am ready for battle.
> I'm ready for anything that comes my way.
> Nothing will stop me from giving it my all.
> My spirit will shine through.
> It is unbreakable.
> All the work is done, and no stone has been left unturned.
> This gives me a sense of calmness and composure.
> I have prepared as best I can.
> I take confidence from my preparation.
> I'm going to be laser-focused on the process, on the ball.
> Nothing else matters.

> As much as this means to me and as much effort I've put in, I remind myself again that this is just a game.
> A game I love, a game I grew up playing as a hobby.
> So I'm going to go out and enjoy myself.
> I'm going to be loose and supple.
> I'm going to be composed under pressure.
> Composure wins the day.
> Now, I will go about my day as normal, my mind empty, my vision clear.
> I will not waste any mental energy thinking about the event.
> I know deep inside what to do.
> I don't need to rehearse or revise anything.

> My instincts and intuition will kick in when it matters, and I trust in them.
> If thoughts or tension arise, I will let them flow through me.
> I will do some 4-by-4 boxed breaths.
> I have all the tools to deal with anything that might distract me.
> Today is going to be a good day. I can feel it.
> Go out, express yourself, and enjoy it.

Post-Game Reflection

~ The game is over.

~ Whether I won or lost, I know I gave it my all.

~ If things went well, I will keep this momentum going.

~ If things did not go well, I will dust myself off and go again.

~ I will learn from my mistakes.

~ Maybe you performed well, but the team lost, or vice versa.

~ You win, or you learn in life.

If you won or things went your way

~ I will reflect on this victory, on this good performance.

~ I will allow myself to feel good about it and linger in that feeling.

~ But I will let it go. I will let it flow through me.

~ It's easy to let the ego suck you into thinking you are great now.

~ It's easy to get comfortable.

~ To think I have it all figured out.

~ It's easy to get complacent.

~ That is what a weak character would do.

~ But I am no weak character.

~ I told myself I would be ready for anything.

~ I enjoy the good days, but I know there are tougher days to come.

~ I will keep this momentum going.

~ I will continue to get stronger and better every day.

~ This is just the beginning.

*****if you lost, or things didn't go your way*****

~ From here, it's easy to give up. It's easy to think *I'm not good enough*.

~ It's easy to think nothing works, no matter how hard I try.

~ No matter how focused I am or how prepared I am.

~ I realize that failure is inevitable.

~ Failure is a part of the journey. It's also a part of winning.

~ This is the universe testing my resolve.

~ If I quit now, I am giving in.

~ Learning curves have bumps and dips along the way.

~ I'm going to dust myself down and go again tomorrow.

~ Reflect on what went wrong.

~ It could be a simple shift in attitude that changes everything.

~ No top athlete in the world that's ever lived has not gone through what I'm going through right now.

~ But it's how they reacted that made them great.

~ Do I want to be great?

~ This is a long journey.

~ I might perform poorly ten more times, but on the eleventh try, everything will click.

~ All the pain and suffering will be worth it.

~ I may feel bad now, but tomorrow is a new day, and I will go again.

~ Nothing can stop my drive, my will.

SECTION 2 – THE JOURNEY

Day 1 – Choose Your Hard

◊   There is a great phrase in life that you should say to yourself as often as possible.

◊   And that is, choose your hard.

◊   First of all, you need to realize that, for the most part, life is hard. It is not easy.

◊   Life's not fair. It never was, and it never will be.

◊   If life were easy, there would be no fun, no joy, and no sense of achievement at the end of a struggle.

◊   Don't get sucked into the victim mentality.

◊   Now let's talk about what's hard about life.

◊   It's hard to be disciplined.

◊   It's hard to stay focused and motivated.

◊   It's hard to hustle and grind late at night when everyone else is watching TV or partying.

◊   It's hard to have a good diet.

◊   It's also hard to be unfit!

◊   It's hard to have health issues.

◊   It's hard not to reach your full potential.

◊   It's hard not to follow your dreams.

◊   It's hard to live in regret.

◊   It's hard to procrastinate.

◊   It's hard to waste your talent away.

◊   Realize this.

***

◊   People talk about how it's hard to be consistent.

◊   It's hard to follow a morning routine.

◊   It's hard to find the time to meditate. To look after your mental health.

◊   It's also hard to be INconsistent!

◊   It's hard to have no routine.

◊   It's hard to be depressed.

◊   It's hard to be governed by the negative chatter in your head.

◊   It's hard to have anxiety.

◊   It's all hard.

◊   So choose your hard!

***

◊   Marriage is hard. Divorce is hard.

◊   Relationships are hard. Being single is hard.

◊   Having kids is hard. Not having kids is hard.

◊ Getting rich and making money is hard. Hustling is hard.

◊ Not giving up is hard.

◊ Failing over and over again is hard.

◊ It's also hard being broke. It's hard to be poor.

◊ It's hard to struggle to make ends meet.

◊ It's hard to give up!

◊ It's hard to have no motivation. No drive. No purpose.

◊ You're either going to work for it and keep getting back up.

◊ Or let life knock you down and live in the victim mentality.

◊ It's all hard in life. No matter what you do.

◊ So before you begin this journey, you need to **choose, your, hard.**

***

◊ You need to realize that you know those times you feel bad for no reason.

◊ You don't know why, but your mood is low.

◊ It's because your subconscious knows you could be doing better.

◊ It knows you're not reaching your potential.

◊ It knows you're not even trying.

◊ That doesn't mean you have to instantly succeed to feel better.

◊ It just means you have to try. You have to move in that direction.

◊ You keep doing that, and soon enough, you'll find yourself feeling good for no reason.

◊ So make a choice.

◊ Choose your hard.

Day 2 – Comeback Season

> This is my year.
> This is my season.
> This is my time.
> I'm going to turn everything around.
> I'm going to show up every day and every night.
> I'm going to put in the work.
> Nothing can stop me.
> Nothing can get in the way of my dream.
> This year, I will be unstoppable.
> No matter what obstacle I face in becoming the best version of myself, I will overcome it.
> I welcome the dark days, the days where I get knocked down, where I'm hurt, where I feel like giving up.
> These days are the most powerful, the most character-building of all.
> These are the days when I KNOW I am ALIVE inside.

> *'the darker the night, the brighter the stars,'* as the great Russian philosopher Fyodor Dostoevsky once said.
> The hurt, the frustration, and the pain only show me that there is a deep burning desire inside me.
> A relentless pursuit of becoming better every day.
> Knock me down 9 times. I get up 10.
> Actually, knock me down 100 times, and I'll get up a thousand.
> That is my mindset.
> Rock solid.
> You cannot beat someone with that mindset.
> You cannot beat someone who never quits.
> Bad days and nights of training will come and go. The next day I will dust myself off and go again.
> Nothing can stop my drive, my spirit.
> When I notice someone doubting me, I smile to myself.
> If they only knew what was burning inside me.
> Let them all doubt. It's going to make my rise all the sweeter.
> I will show them.
> But I will not make proving other people wrong my main focus.
> Oftentimes, people get too hung up on proving their doubters wrong.
> While it's important to use that energy as motivation, it's not my main focus.

> My focus is laser-like, I have tunnel vision, and my eyes are on the prize of glory.
> I know where I'm heading, and that is to the top.
> When I succeed, the doubters will be the least of my concern. Proving them wrong will be a by-product of my success.
> I rise above it all.
> You don't have time to look back when you're climbing to the top of the mountain.
> I am ecstatic about the year.
> Bring it on.

Day 3 – Misunderstood

- o Some people will not understand this journey I'm on.
- o They simply won't get it.
- o I may lose some friends or so-called friends along the way.
- o I may have family questioning me or worrying about me.
- o People will begin to notice a difference in me.
- o I'm not going to parties as much. I'm not staying up watching Netflix every night.
- o I've got something else in my mind, a vision of the future.
- o This will make some people uncomfortable because I'm being different.
- o I'm acting differently.
- o That's because I'm looking for a different outcome than the same old predictable one.
- o Einstein said, *"Insanity is doing the same thing over and over and expecting different results."*

o While it's easy to be upset or disappointed in friends who are not supportive.

o Know that it's just a weakness on their end. They have yet to be inspired to make a change.

o Some may end up being inspired by my actions.

o Either way, I will show compassion and empathy.

o They are on their own journey and will find their way eventually.

o I don't need to drop these friends unless it's becoming toxic and distracting me.

o In those cases, those friends were not true friends in the first place.

o I don't waste my time on social media anymore.

o Comparing my life to others, mindlessly scrolling to pass the time.

o I don't gossip or give out about petty things.

o I don't have the time to think about any of that.

o It's not on my radar.

o I begin to realize how much mental energy I have been wasting on pointless things for years.

o Instead, I'm reading books. I'm listening to podcasts. I'm learning.

o I'm reacting differently to life situations.

o There is a new energy about me.

o A pep in my step.

o A clearer look in my eyes.

o A look of clarity, of assertiveness.

o Strangers begin to respond to me differently.

o Animals and dogs come up to me in the street.

o They can read my energy.

o   Signs and synchronicities start popping up out of nowhere.
o   I no longer give in to short-term pleasures, be it junk food, Netflix binges, or pointless nights out.
o   I pick and choose when to do these things. I do them in moderation. As a reward for the work I've put in.
o   But in general, I delay the pleasure for a more long-term pursuit.
o   I begin to feel good for no reason.
o   I know it's my subconscious telling me I'm on the right path.

Day 4 – The Puma / Stealth Mode

ø I am reaching new levels, both mentally and physically.

ø I can feel the improvements in my game day by day.

ø I'm becoming more resilient to life's challenges and setbacks.

ø I'm beginning to understand that they are all part of the journey of improvement.

ø I'm beginning to understand what it takes to be great.

ø I'm no longer reacting off emotion after a good performance or a bad one.

ø I'm no longer feeling sorry for myself when I lose or get complacent when I win.

ø I stay humble.

ø I keep chipping away at perfecting my skills, day by day, sharpening my tools.

ø I'm biding my time and waiting for my opportunity to strike.

ø Like a puma stalking its prey through the bushes.

ø   Pumas often stalk their prey from a distance.

ø   Lurking in the tall grass, carefully following for an hour or even longer.

ø   In stealth mode.

ø   Waiting for the right moment to pounce and crush their victim.

ø   They don't lose composure. They don't attack too soon.

ø   When the time is right, they will sneak up from behind and catch their prey off guard.

ø   Ensuring the kill, giving themselves every opportunity for success.

ø   People often talk about playing the percentages in sports and in business.

ø   And that's exactly what a puma does.

ø   One rushed attack too soon, one wrong move in the bushes…

ø   And the attack is over, the prey gets away, and food is delayed.

ø   It's the way of the animal kingdom.

ø   This is why the puma gives itself every chance to succeed.

ø   Powerfully leaping on their target's back. Suffocating it within seconds.

ø   Much like a puma, I know my opportunity will come.

ø   I won't be shouting from the rooftops about what I plan to do.

ø   I stay composed and still.

ø   When game day comes, when the opportunity arises.

ø   I am ready to pounce. I am ready to perform.

ø   Not just for the prey but for the puma also; this is life or death.

ø   It could mean feasting now or not eating for days.

ø   That is why their concentration is at a maximum.

ø   There are no outside distractions or thoughts.

ø   Pure focus and flow state.

ø   And that is how I play.

ø   No distractions, clarity of mind.

ø   Totally focused and concentrated on the process, on the next ball, the next race, the next performance.

ø   When I play like this, pure skill takes over.

ø   I get out of my own way.

ø   Most people fold under pressure.

ø   But I have prepared myself for all obstacles on this journey.

ø   In the end, my composure will make the difference, just like the pumas.

Day 5 – Cementing Greatness

~ I train like a beast. That's how I enjoy it.

~ I am laser-focused on winning.

~ I can run faster and jump higher than anyone.

~ My endurance is through the roof. I can outlast anybody.

~ I am a born winner.

~ I am faster than lightning.

~ I love the feeling of competing.

~ Through repetition and never giving up, I achieve my full athletic potential.

~ I am a highly-skilled athlete in all areas.

~ I am a weapon, and I am always improving, like sharpening a blade.

~ Motivation comes easily to me.

~ Even on days when I am not motivated, I know that 10 minutes into my warm-up, when the sweat is pumping and the heart rate is up, my motivation will be ever-present.

~ This is what I live for. That adrenaline. That rush.

~ I'm beginning to enjoy this feeling.

~ With hard work, I naturally achieve all my athletic goals.

~ I push myself to the edge of my skill level, to the edge of my comfort zone, and to the edge of my fitness. That is where progress happens.

~ I test myself mentally and physically every day.

~ I don't burn out. I take rest days when I need to.

~ I listen to my body.

~ I raise the standards of my game every day.

~ I am confident in my ability.

~ I stay focused under pressure like a navy seal.

~ I am on top of my game now.

~ I walk around with my shoulders back and my chest out.

~ Nothing can stop me.

~ Nothing can throw me off focus.

~ I'm a completely new person now.

~ It's having a ripple effect on other areas of my life too.

~ Everything seems to be falling into place.

~ I was born to do this.

~ I was born to be a champion.

Day 6 – Demon Time / The Doubts

- Even though I am on top of my game, doubts can still creep in.
- Some days I don't feel motivated.
- Some setbacks hit harder than others.
- Sometimes I begin to question everything.
- Devastating injuries can happen.
- Huge losses in form can happen.
- No matter how well I'm going, I'm only as good as my last game or performance. That's all people remember.
- Despite all my hard work and all my progress, I'm still feeling uncertain.
- Why is this?
- Just when everything seemed to be falling into place, something has thrown me off path.
- A bad run of games. An unlucky injury just when my fitness was peaking.
- These things can and will happen in a season.
- I'm experiencing what is known as *'The Dip.'*

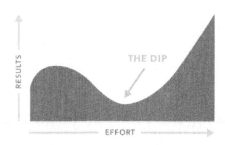

-

- The dip is where, after all your initial efforts, you begin to see progress in results, and then, suddenly, there is this huge dip. This occurs in all aspects of life, be it business or sport.
- I've heard of this before but never experienced it.
- How can I feel like this after all the progress I've made? After all the work I've put in?
- Now the old familiar demons are coming back to haunt me:

- *'I'm not good enough for this level'*
- *'I've sacrificed all this time for nothing'*
- *'My old coaches were right when they said I wouldn't make it'*
- *'My body is too weak, too slow. I'm getting injured too easily'*
- *'it's too hard, it's too difficult, it's not worth it'*
- *'I shouldn't have tried in the first place. It was stupid'*

- **'Maybe I'm just not good enough or it's not meant to be'**
- **'Maybe I'm not mentally tough enough'**

***

- I'm so far into this journey and now I suddenly find myself at a crossroads.
- Just last week, I was feeling on top of the world.
- Have I become mentally weak?
- I need to realize that this is possibly the most critical part of this journey.
- There's a saying that the devil only comes when you are doing something right.
- This is make-or-break time.
- This is what separates the good from the great.
- Most people quit and fall off after the dip.
- But those who make it past the dip can reach new levels never before experienced.
- I need to figure this out and get over this hurdle.
- I've put my life and soul into this pursuit.
- I'm going to hang in there just a little while longer and see what happens...

Day 7 – Inspiration from History

Here we are going to discuss some of the setbacks and adversities that faced the greatest people of history who changed the world. These are not affirmations but short stories.

Nikola Tesla

The man who invented alternating current, the same form of electricity we use today, lighting up the world, faced many setbacks on his path. First, he contracted cholera as a teenager. He was bedridden for nine months and on death's door. His father, who originally wanted Nikola to follow him into the priesthood, promised to send him to the best engineering school possible if he recovered.

Tesla recovered, but soon after, war broke out in Austria. Being of fighting age, he fled to the mountains to avoid being called upon. Here he explored the mountains and nature, reading tons of books. He eventually went to college, only to develop a gambling addiction. He gambled all his tuition money away and lost all contact with his family.

Finally, he got his act together and began moving up in his career; such was his talent and intelligence. He made his way to work with the Edison company in the US. He showed Thomas Edison himself some designs of improved versions of the DC motor but was dismissed.

He decided to set up his own electrical company, but his investors screwed him out of all his money and claimed the patents of his profitable inventions. To make ends meet, for some time after that, he was forced to dig ditches for $2 a day.

- Creating perhaps one of the most important inventions in world history and literally changing the world for the better, Nikola Tesla's path was not easy.
- He could have given up many times on his journey.
- Time and again, he fought back from adversity and hardship where many others would have given in.
- Brought back to life in recent times thanks to Elon Musk, Tesla will forever be immortalized.
- His intelligence and skill would have come to nothing were it not for his sheer determination and perseverance.

Joan of Arc

In the 1400s, aged just 13, a young peasant French girl named Jeanne claimed to have powerful visions from angels instructing her to drive the English out of France for good. They had taken over most of northern France at the time.

At 16, she found help from a relative to speak to a lower-ranked French commander. She pleaded with the commander to give her an armed escort to the royal court for an audience with the French King, King Charles VII. Being instantly dismissed, she appealed to the commander's soldiers and made a unique prediction on what would happen in the war in the near future. Her unlikely predictions came through, and the French commander was now a reluctant believer. He granted her request. At 17, she met with the King.

From there, she made many more predictions and was brought into strategic military meetings, advising on how to win crucial battles. She then became a commander and led her soldiers to many important victories with her aggressive, offensive tactics, helping to drive the English out of France and saving many innocent French lives. Her mysticism and fame continued to grow after her death. Her name lives on.

- In a time in history where a woman's opinion meant little to nothing, for a teenage peasant girl to get an audience with the king was wild in itself.
- But to then go on to give strategic advice and lead armies to important victories is nothing short of amazing.
- Were it not for her willpower and belief in her own convictions, her home country could have suffered a far worse fate.

Victor E Frankl

Victor Frankl was a Jewish holocaust survivor who spent 3 years in a concentration camp in Auschwitz during World War 2, run by German Nazis. He lost his wife and most of his family at the time. He saw men die every day from disease and mistreatment. He was faced with the most horrific of situations a man could ever face. Yet still, he refused to give up hope.

- He said that *'everything can be taken from a man but one thing, the last of the human freedoms, to choose one's attitude in any given set of circumstances.*

- He also said, *'those who have a why to live can bear with almost any how'.*

- He then wrote one of the most powerful and impactful books ever written, 'Mans *Search for Meaning.*

- He also developed a type of therapy called logotherapy which centered around everything he experienced.

- Through his therapy, he helped thousands of people find meaning in their life and a reason to live on through their suffering. Truly inspirational.

There are hundreds, if not thousands, of examples throughout history where people were faced with huge adversities yet persevered through it all to come out the other side. Look to the past at any great achievement, and you will find that each one came with obstacles that seemed impossible to overcome at the time.

■■

These accounts were inspired by the book series **'20 Game Changers in History'.**

If you would like to learn more, the book is available here>>>

20 Game Changers in History

Book QR code:

The Audiobook is also available for **free** *with Audible.>>*

Audiobook QR code:

Day 8 - Spirit and Perseverance

◊ My spirit has been tested to the limit, but it cannot be broken.

◊ My will is too strong.

◊ I've gone to hell and back.

◊ So I won't be stopped now.

◊ I am made of steel.

◊ I can and will be triumphant.

◊ No matter how long it takes to achieve my goal, I know I will get there.

◊ My belief in my ability has never been stronger after what I've been through.

◊ More importantly, my belief in my own resolve and strength of character has shown me that I've got what it takes.

◊ My time has come.

◊ Despite all the doubts. All the familiar demons I've faced time and time again.

◊ I'm still standing.

◊ I'm still showing up, day after day, night after night—a relentless pursuit of greatness.

◊ Pursuing greatness in and of itself is one of the noblest things a person or an athlete can do.

◊ It's something I take pride in.

◊ It's you versus you.

◊ I'm competing with the person in the mirror.

◊ I've gone to war with myself, with my ego, with my doubts.

◊ And I've come out the other side.

◊ Persevering through the tough times makes the good times all the sweeter.

◊ Now my belief in myself is more apparent than ever.

◊ My mental toughness cannot be broken.

◊ My skill is exceptional.

◊ I have amazing speed and endurance.

◊ I am an outstanding athlete.

◊ I am a leader.

◊ I was born to do this.

◊ Performing under pressure comes easily to me.

◊ I enjoy it and look forward to the pressure.

◊ I look forward to the different tests I may face.

◊ My heart, my will, and my spirit cannot be broken.

◊ They are what makes me great.

◊ They are what make me a champion.

Day 9 – Judgement Day

> Finally, the big day has come.

> I can feel the nervous energy.

> But unlike before, when I would bottle it up. Now I let it flow through me.

> I convert that energy into excitement.

> I welcome it in.

> I can breathe and do the boxed breaths whenever I need to center myself.

> I don't waste mental energy worrying about the game's finer details.

> I'm too experienced now.

> I trust my intuition to make the right decision at the right time.

> I trust my composure.

> My preparation gives me confidence.

> I have left no stone unturned.

> I've overcome every obstacle thrown my way.

> I've faced all my demons and come out the other side.

> Today nothing can stop me.
> Win, lose or draw, I know I will give all I have.
> My character will shine through in any difficult times.
> Hard work and honesty are the foundation of my game.
> Once I bring those two attributes, the rest will take care of itself.
> Just like the puma, my concentration will be at a maximum.
> Laser-focused on the process.
> All distractions will be eliminated.
> My mind is clear, in a state of flow.
> I am ready to have the game of my life.
> Today is going to be a good day.
> My spirits are high.
> I am a top-level athlete.
> I have all the skills in the world.
> I am powerful and strong, both mentally and physically.
> Nothing can stop me.
> The time for talking is done.
> Now it's time for action.
> The hard part is over.
> Now it's about going out and expressing myself.
> And most importantly, enjoying myself.
> This I what I love to do.
> I will relax from now until the game starts.

> I am excited and ready to showcase my skill.
> To showcase my resolve. My mental toughness.
> Today is the day I come of age.

Day 10 – Reflecting Back

- ø The journey is over.
- ø I went after greatness, and I achieved it.
- ø Whether I won my competition, my event, or not.
- ø My greatness was achieved in its pursuit, in striving for it.
- ø Outside accolades and accomplishments are well and good.
- ø But what I accomplished inside of me is the most rewarding achievement of all.
- ø I now know what it takes, and I know I have it in me.
- ø I take huge pride in the mountain I've climbed.
- ø Facing every obstacle possible, I persevered.
- ø Through all the doubts and all the ups and downs, I came out the other side.
- ø I am a new person with a new perspective on everything.
- ø I am filled with pride in myself.
- ø I am filled with passion.

- ø My skill and mental toughness have reached levels I didn't know were possible.
- ø I am now ready for anything life throws my way.
- ø I've had a taste of success, and I'm hungry for more.
- ø This is just the beginning.
- ø I'm going to go from strength to strength.
- ø I wasn't sure if it was going to be worthwhile.
- ø Sacrificing so much time, missing out on certain events.
- ø Forcing myself to have daily discipline.
- ø Forcing myself to get back up every time I fell down.
- ø Overpowering my inner demons and doubts with sheer will and self-talk.
- ø But it was absolutely worth it.
- ø I've proven to myself that I can get through anything.
- ø I feel invincible.
- ø This feeling is addictive.
- ø The feeling of progress is addictive.
- ø I want to achieve more.
- ø I want to accomplish more.
- ø This has opened my eyes to what's possible.
- ø I have limitless potential.
- ø Anything I put my mind to, I can achieve.
- ø Whether it's in work, sports, or relationships, it does not matter.

- ∅ I have grown so much and learned so much about myself.
- ∅ I'm so happy and fulfilled that I went after my dream.
- ∅ I can't wait to do it all again.
- ∅ I'm as motivated as ever.
- ∅ I now understand the power of self-talk, the power of the mind.
- ∅ I understand it on a deep level, not just superficially.
- ∅ I will rest up now and take a break.
- ∅ But I'm already looking forward to getting back to work.
- ∅ This is just the beginning.

Before we conclude with the final bonus section, I want to thank you for reading this book and I hope it brought you some inspiration. If you found this book helpful, I would greatly appreciate if you could take 30 seconds to write a brief review on Amazon. A sentence or two will do. That way, it will help like-minded people find this book. The provided QR code will take you straight to the review section.

*(If Based in the UK or elsewhere, simply edit the **'.com'** to **'.co.uk'** or whatever relevant country code after you scan the QR code.)*

Thank you! I like forward to seeing your thoughts.

SECTION 3 – BONUS INTERACTIVE RESOURCES

A - Finding Your Why

Here are some questions that you may need time to think deeply about. The purpose of these questions is to make you truly understand your *'why'*; the core reasons why you play and why you practice. If you can get to the root of your *why and* are happy and content with the answers you find, then you won't lack the motivation to show up and train. If your why is weaker than you thought, it may be time to re-evaluate things.

So grab a pen or pencil. Use a blank sheet of paper if you do not want to write in this book, and find a quiet place where you won't be disturbed.

1. **How did you feel on your first day of playing the sport/hobby/passion you now play? You may not remember exactly, but how do you think you would have felt?**

_____
_____
_____
_____
_____
_____
_____
_____

2. How did you feel when you first tasted success while playing that sport/hobby? You didn't have to win a competition. It could simply be scoring your first important goal, making your first block/tackle, or something that stood out. It could be playing in a competition with people watching. How did you feel at that moment? There's a good chance your love for the game came from these early moments.

_____
_____
_____
_____
_____
_____
_____
_____

3. When did you begin to realize you could be successful in this field? When did you realize this is something you love and want to do for the rest of your life?

_____
_____
_____
_____
_____
_____
_____
_____

4. Are those early memories why you still play today and want to be the best?

_____
_____
_____
_____
_____
_____
_____

5. Now, take your time and truly think deeply about this question. Why do you train so hard today?

_____
_____
_____
_____
_____
_____

_____

_____

If you answered something like:

- I want to be a regional champion
- I want to be successful
- I want recognition for my skills
- I want to feel like a champion
- People will recognize me
- I may become famous or wealthy

Really ask yourself why that is. You're most likely chasing a feeling. Just make sure it's the right one. It could be a feeling of joy, excitement, or fulfillment. There's nothing wrong with chasing money, fame, or recognition. Just be sure you're doing this for yourself first and foremost. Because reaching your full potential, or striving to reach it, will make you feel fulfilled on a deep level. It's something that you will feel on a subconscious level. **So what is that feeling you are chasing?**

_____

_____

_____

_____

_____

_____

_____

_____

If you discover that you're doing this work for the wrong reasons, it may be time to re-evaluate things. Examples of some potential wrong reasons are as follows:

- Because my family always played this sport.
- Because my father has always wanted me to be the best, it was his dream.
- Because if I don't play, my friends won't value me as much.
- It keeps me busy. It's something to do. Even though I don't truly enjoy it

It's worth noting here that there is absolutely nothing wrong with playing a sport to be a part of a team. If you enjoy the camaraderie and team spirit, that is all that matters, even if you don't love the actual sport itself. There are no right or wrong answers here as such. If you are trying to lose weight and are hitting the gym, you may not enjoy working out. But you most likely enjoy the feelings and endorphins you get afterward. You enjoy compliments from family or friends that you look leaner and healthier. And those are noble reasons to continue working out. The payoff is worth it. That also goes for the entrepreneur, who doesn't necessarily love the work but loves the reward, and the financial freedom they are obtaining. This, in turn, may lead to early retirement or taking their family on vacation. Only you will know if you are participating in your field or hobby for the right reasons or not.

***

(The next set of questions is for anyone who realizes their reasons are wrong. This is not actually their passion or dream. This is not making

them happy. They also apply to anyone who is attempting to figure out what their passion is. Skip this section if it does not apply to you.)

1. **Think back to your childhood or teenage years, and list at least 5 sports, hobbies, or activities that gave you joy. (list more than 5 if you please).**

_____

_____

_____

_____

_____

_____

_____

_____

2. **What was it about these activities that you loved? What feelings did they generate?**

_____

_____

_____

_____

_____

_____

_____

_____

3. **Can you turn one of those activities into a passion? Can you join a team or club and get back into it again? So what's stopping you?**

_____

_____

_____

_____

_____

_____

_____

_____

I know people in their fifties and sixties who still play squash and table tennis with clubs. Two or three nights a week, they will play competitive games amongst other members, and the joy they receive from still playing their sport is fantastic. I have played against some of these people in my twenties, and they have schooled me numerous times. And I was often jealous of how much fun they were having.

I've met other people who have said things like '*I used to be a regional champion at that in school*' or '*I used to play that instrument really well*' or '*back in my day, nobody could beat me at X.*' Unfortunately, most people think it's too late, and they can't go back doing what they love. But with today's online world, there are clubs, groups, and communities of like-minded people all across the world. Simply searching groups on Facebook will get you in touch with communities near you that have similar passions.

4. **Finally, what will I do this week to get back involved in that sport or activity?**

(e.g., I'm going to buy a new road bike, basketball hoop, instrument, chessboard, etc.)

***

While it's important to stay disciplined and organized, never forget the carefree love and joy you once had while playing your sport. As they get older, many athletes become too serious and organized and lose their joy and love for the game.

There are two extremes. Yes, you need to train hard, but you also want to maintain that love and joy from simply playing the sport or doing the activity. An example is Steph Curry. While he trains hard, he is having just as much fun shooting 3-pointers in an empty court as he is in front of thousands.

On the other hand, if you are not organized, don't sleep right, don't take care of your diet, or don't bother to warm up and stretch correctly. You may be having fun and enjoying your sport. But sooner or later, injuries will occur, you won't perform at your best, and you won't reach your full potential. If you're playing the sport as a past-time, that's all fine. But to make it to the top, you must combine discipline with having fun.

I hope by now, you have found your *why*.

B – What's Blocking You

The next phase of this journey is figuring out what's getting in the way of your success.

Off the top of your head, write down 5 habits or factors that are blocking you or could potentially block you from reaching your goals.

1._____
2._____
3._____
4._____
5._____

Now, to re-evaluate what a block could be. Let's talk about what you may have answered.

- *"I don't have the time. I work a 9-5. When I get home, I am tired and don't have the energy."*

Is it really because of work? Could this be translated to:

- *"I'm not organized enough to pack my gear and lunch the night before, go to bed slightly earlier, and get up and go to the gym before work by getting up 1 hour earlier. "*

-   *"I'm not willing to go straight from work, and when I get home, I don't have the energy to go back out."*

Another block you may have is something to the effect of:

-   *"I keep getting injured; I keep rolling my ankle. I just have weak ankles and it's preventing me from training and reaching my potential."*
    (insert whatever injury you chose)

Could this be translated to:

-   *"I have a weakness in my ankles, and I'm not prepared to warm-up up and stretch them correctly before every training. I'm not willing to strap it up and do the rehabilitation exercises my physio recommended. It's too much effort. It's boring."*

Another block could be:

-   *"Because I don't have the energy and always feel rundown. I get sick often. It's outside of my control."*

Could you translate this to:

-   *"I stay on my phone too late most nights. I don't take vitamins or eat a healthy breakfast*

> *in the mornings, which in turn leaves me*
> *feeling tired and sick from time to time."*

I think you get the point that all of these blocks are within your control. And I'm sure if you have read through the affirmations, you have realized that the days of feeling like a victim in life are over. If they are not, it's time to put an end to them—no more blaming circumstances for getting in the way of your success.

Other potential blocks could be:

- *I'm afraid of failure.*
- *I'm not disciplined enough*
- *I'm afraid of what people will think if I don't succeed.*
- *I don't want to end my social life.*
- *I don't believe I am good enough.*

These are all limiting beliefs that you need to work on and let go of. I suggest doing some inner work. That could be in the form of mediation or using the letting go technique, which I highly recommend. Letting Go is a book by David R Hawkins. It's about letting go of emotions, traumas, and limiting beliefs using a simple technique. This is essentially a form of self-therapy. You may even want to look into therapy in general.

Any way you can improve your self-esteem and let go of limiting beliefs will help you on your journey to success. Mediation and letting go can clear your mind of old repetitive thought processes. They can clear your body of old traumas and emotions which are stuck and want to be released. This allows space for new ideas, new beliefs, and emotions to come in. Sports and passions aside, this works wonders on your overall well-being and state of mind. You will actually feel lighter as a result, no longer carrying the weight of the world on your shoulders.

Get clear on your why. Get clear on your blocks. And finally, realize that it's all in your control and make a commitment to no longer be a victim.

So now, be totally honest with yourself, and write down your blocks again—your true blocks. Don't be ashamed of what you write, for this level of honesty is a true sign of strength. And many people can't bring themselves to do this, which is why they keep getting mediocre results.

You will now have a clear idea of what you need to work on.

1._____

2._____

3._____

4._____

5._____

C – Visualization Exercises

Visualization, when done correctly, is a potent tool for any successful entrepreneur or athlete. It primes your body and mind for what's possible. Nearly every top athlete and sports team practices visualization. The same goes for top entrepreneurs and businesses. They envision what success looks and feels like BEFORE achieving it. Sports psychologists and life coaches have become extremely valuable members of teams and companies in recent years.

Most people visualize on autopilot. And those visualizations consist of thinking up negative scenarios about the past or future. The mind is built to survive, so anticipating any perceived negative events is done to protect you from danger. But the problem is that people are stuck in this fight or flight response mode all day, despite not being in direct danger. And this is leading to many mental health and anxiety problems in today's society. By anticipating the worst outcomes, you are putting extra stress and pressure on the body and mind.

So if you do not become AWARE of your thoughts. AWARE of your thinking process. Your mind goes into auto-pilot and mainly thinks of negative thoughts. However, if you CONSCIOUSLY become aware of the thoughts in your head, refuse to give them energy or attention, and just let them flow through you. You are now taking back control.

After doing this, if you can consciously think of positive thoughts and visualizations to replace the negative ones, you are well on your way to mastering your mind and realizing those visualizations.

Now it's time to move on to the visualization exercises. I will allow time for you to think deeply about and feel the visualization. So again, find a quiet space where you will not be disturbed. I also recommend doing some short box-breathing cycles to relax and close your eyes after you have read through what to visualize.

Visualization 1 - Your 5-year-old self

- I want you to visualize your earliest memory of joy playing any sport or doing any activity. It could be the memories you listed earlier, but it doesn't have to be. It also doesn't have to be while playing the sport or hobby you do now.
- Think back and put your awareness into the younger version of yourself at that moment. How did you feel? What were you thinking? What worries did you have at that time while playing? What positive feelings did you experience?
- Visualize the whole scene. Think about the sounds, the weather, the voices of other people there, and the smell in the air. Sit with it and go through it for 5-10 minutes.

*** 10-minute pause***

Now that you have returned from this visualization experience, write down 5 or 10 things that stood out to you. What emotions did you feel? What did you miss about that time or about that version of you? Did it excite you to potentially make a change?
Write down whatever notes you need.

_____
_____
_____
_____
_____
_____
_____
_____
_____
_____
_____
_____
_____
_____
_____
_____

Visualization 2 – Achieving Greatness

- Firstly, go ahead and do some box breathing again or whatever technique you like to help you relax back into that calm state. Find a quiet place where you won't be disturbed.
- Now I want you to visualize yourself achieving your dream. I want you to imagine this highest version of yourself.

- I want you to mainly focus on the state and feeling you would be in AFTER you achieve your dream. So if that is winning a basketball championship, don't focus on the details of the final game. Focus on the winning feeling AFTER the game. The locker room scenes. Meeting your family and friends all congratulating you.
- Maybe you're lifting a trophy for an event or individual sport.
- Maybe it's the feeling of being 10 kg lighter in 3 or 6 months from now. Think about how that would feel. Visualize meeting your family and friends and receiving those compliments. Picture yourself walking down the street with a new confidence and purpose.
- The important thing here is to not worry about HOW you are going to achieve this. Just focus on the feelings OF achieving it.
- So whatever your dream is, try to imagine the feelings after achieving your dream. Think of the scenes, the sounds, the atmospheres, and the people you meet.
- I will now allow you 10 minutes to sit with these images and feelings.

*** 10-minute pause***

Now that you have come back from this visualization experience, write down 5 or 10 things that stood out. What emotions did you feel? Who did you see or speak to? What was the atmosphere like? How did you feel

inside? Did it excite you? Did it inspire you to do everything to make this vision a reality?

_____
_____
_____
_____
_____
_____
_____
_____
_____
_____
_____
_____
_____
_____
_____
_____
_____

Visualization 3 – If you do NOT go after your passion or dream

- Finally, get into a relaxed state again and this time, visualize some time in the future and what that would look like if you do nothing. If you keep doing what you've always been doing.
- Picture 6 months or 2 years from now, and you haven't gone after your dream or made any big changes to your day-to-day life.
- How will your life look?
- What scenes can you visualize?
- What people are you hanging around with?

- What kind of results are you getting in your chosen sport/interest?
- Are you satisfied with your situation?
- Can you see other people getting ahead and achieving great results in their life that you could have achieved?
- Sit with all and allow any images and feelings to come up. I'll allow 10 minutes for you to do this exercise.

*** 10-minute pause***

Now that you have come back from this visualization experience, write down 5 or 10 things that stood out. What emotions did you feel? Who did you see or speak to? What was the atmosphere like? How did you feel inside? Were you disappointed? Write down whatever comes to mind.

_____

_____

_____

_____

_____

_____

_____

_____

_____

_____

_____

_____

_____ _____
_____ _____
_____ _____

I hope these visualization exercises have lit an even bigger fire inside you and opened your mind to what's possible. The first visualization may have served as a reminder of just how much fun you used to have. Perhaps you were more carefree at the time and were enjoying yourself a lot more. It's always good to remind yourself of that child-like state.

Visualization 3 is something I recommend doing only sometimes, but it can serve as a huge wake-up call and shock to the system whenever you feel yourself slacking off. Many people are motivated by the fear of failure or the fear of letting themselves down. So seeing your future play out if you don't make any changes is crucial. You won't want to let yourself down like that, especially when you know you can do better.

Most people never do these types of exercises and so don't realize what's possible for them. Visualization 2 may have produced images in your mind that you didn't think were possible. But just remember Napoleon Hill's famous words:

"Whatever Your Mind Can Conceive and Believe, It Can Achieve."

If you can see that image of yourself succeeding and thriving, then it's possible. The more you practice visualizing, the clearer these images will be, and the greater your motivation will be. I hope these exercises served their purpose, and I strongly encourage you to visualize your dream becoming a reality as often as possible. It's only going to benefit you and provide more motivation and drive to strive for that goal.

D – The Habit Builder

It's important to figure out what habits you can introduce into your everyday life to aid you in achieving your goal. Habit is such an overused word nowadays, and people often overcomplicate its true meaning. While you can have all the aspirations and dreams in the world, unless you start building new daily habits, you most likely won't realize that dream.

Another problem with building habits going too big. Like how gyms are packed every January and empty by February. People who go from doing nothing for months to promising themselves they'll hit the gym for an hour four nights a week for the next six months. They may keep it up for three or four weeks, but then they give up. You have to make incremental, sustainable changes and habits. Otherwise, you won't maintain them. It's why most diets don't work. They are unsustainable.

What is a Habit?
Put simply, a habit is something you do every day or at least a few times a week. A habit is also more or less the same action, the same routine, and the same thought process. If you eat cookies every day after dinner, that's a habit. If you brush your teeth for two minutes each morning, that's also a habit. You need to think of some new habits you can

implement into your daily life that will help you achieve your goal.

So if your goal is to lose 10 kg next three months. And you currently haven't worked out or eaten right in months. A realistic habit may be:

- ***I'm going to walk 10'000 steps every day.***

  Or

- ***I'm going to sign up for a PT or fitness class and go 1-2 times a week.***

Something unrealistic for that scenario is:

- ***I'm going to start a new morning routine and get up at 6 am every morning and go for a 10 km run.***

- ***I'm going to reduce my calories by 900 a day and hit the gym four times a week.***

If you are an elite athlete who has a tight back and is feeling run down, A new habit may be:

- ***I'm going to do 20 mins of yoga every morning and before practice to ensure my back is loose.***

- ***I'm going to take multivitamins each morning and get 8 hours of sleep.***

The important thing to remember is that it's ok if you miss a day here or there as long as you get back on the horse and don't let it be 2 or 3 days in a row.

James Clear, the author of *Atomic Habits*, explains how by simply making a calender and marking an X on the days you do your habit or task, you are giving yourself a dopamine hit and will be compelled to maintain these streaks and not miss two days in a row. This activity in itself is an amazing habit and can be great for anyone who struggles to stay disciplined.

Depending on your journey or goal, examples of daily habits could be as follows:

- *Practicing the piano for 15 minutes every day*
- *Packing my gym gear the night before*
- *Meditating for 10 minutes every morning*
- *Drinking 2 liters of water a day for more energy*
- *Practicing shooting on my weaker foot for 20 minutes after every soccer practice*

If you're an entrepreneur could be:

- *I'm going to turn my phone on silent and work for 1 hour every evening on my side project*
- *I'm going to come to my boss with solutions to problems he and the company are facing*

So now that you understand what type of habits you can implement and how to monitor your progress, it's time to list them out.

First, write down your overall goal/dream/ambition.

_____
_____
_____
_____
_____

**Now, list out 5 – 10 simple habits you think you could
implement every day to help you achieve your dream
(you won't be doing all 5 or 10)**

_____
_____
_____
_____
_____
_____
_____
_____
_____
_____
_____
_____
_____
_____

Circle one or two of the most important ones and commit
to doing those every day. It's also crucial that you track
your progress. Make it manageable at the start, even if
that's just 10 or 15 minutes of the given habit. Slowly over

time, you can build on this and increase the time or the number of habits.

Here is what a simple calendar tracker can look like with the Xs filled in. Stick it up in your room and mark an X every day you complete your habit. And try not to let consecutive blank days build up. It's a good idea to make them into four or six week blocks and then reassess the situation from there.

It may not seem like much progress, but six weeks of 15 minutes of practice of an instrument will have you much closer to perfecting it than you think. That goes for any skill or habit you are working on. Suppose you commit to a habit of packing your gym gear before going to bed and getting up 45 minutes earlier every morning. It will soon feel effortless, and you will have racked up way more gym sessions per week, leaving you feeling healthier and better about yourself.

M	T	W	T	F	S	S	
X	X		X	X		X	Week 1
X	X	X	X	X			Week 2
X	X	X	X		X		Week 3
X		X	X	X		X	Week 4
	X	X	X			X	Week 5
X	X	X	X	X		X	Week 6

E – Box Breathing

Box breathing is a great technique to use in many situations, such as:

- Coping with anxiety and stress when you are feeling overwhelmed. Counting helps to take the focus away from the situation that's causing you stress which enables you to control your response.
- Sleep trouble. It helps you get to sleep easier if you suffer from insomnia.
- Small panic attacks. It can assist in controlling hyperventilation as you are instructing your lungs to breathe rhythmically.
- Helps you refocus and get back into the present moment if you are having a busy or stressful day.
- Eases the mind and any overthinking and worry.
- Keeps you calm while preparing for the day or event
- When you have a big decision to make. It clears the mind.
- Improving your mood. Box breathing can Lower blood pressure and decreases Cortisol — a stress hormone — which can improve your overall mood.

Where can you Practice Box Breathing?

The main benefit of box breathing is that you can practice it anywhere, anytime. Whether that's before a game, at work, at home, in your car, or in any stressful situation. Just be aware that you don't have to practice box breathing only when feeling stressed. It's a fantastic habit to build and you can do it to calm your mind and body. It can act as a reset button for your mood at any time of the day.

Best Practice for Box Breathing

- Sit in a comfortable seat, stand, or lie down on your back with one hand on your stomach and the other on your chest. When you sit on a chair, ensure that your back is supported and your feet are firmly on the ground.
- Breathe normally for one minute.
- Observe the movement of your chest and stomach as you breathe
- If you are breathing through your chest, this is shallow breathing. You want to breathe through your stomach and diaphragm. This is deep breathing which helps the body relax. You may have always been shallow breathing and if so, it's a good idea to work on this habit as often as possible.
- Be aware of your breath to ensure that you are taking deep breaths, allowing your stomach to rise and fall.
- If you are sitting or lying down, you should feel your back pressed against the surface when you take a deep breath with your stomach.

- If this is your first time practicing box breathing, push your stomach out while focusing on smooth, deep breaths.

It's advised to practice deep breathing as often as possible.

The guided box breathing meditation is available on the next page.

>>>

Box Breathing Guided Mediation

Now, once you are ready to begin, close your eyes.

It helps to visualize a square in your mind. So as you breathe in through your nose and fill your diaphragm, picture one side of a square being drawn or highlighted.

As you hold and breathe out through your mouth, visualize the next sides of the square, and so on.

- Count to four as you inhale.

- Breath in...two, three, four.

- Now, hold your breath for a count of four.

- Hold...two, three, four.

- Then open your mouth slowly, and slowly exhale a count of four.

- Out...two, three, four.

- Now, hold the exhale to another count of four. Pause...two, three, four.

We are going to do this exercise for 5 full minutes accounting for 15 boxed breaths. So let's go again-

- Count to four as you inhale.

- Breath in...two, three, four.

- Now, hold your breath for a count of four.

- Hold...two, three, four.

- Slowly exhale out...two, three, four.

- Pause...two, three, four.

- Again, breathe in...two, three, four.

- Hold...two, three, four.

- Exhale...two, three, four.

- Pause...two, three, four.

3. Breathe in...two, three, four. - Hold...two, three, four. - exhale...two, three, four. - Pause...two, three, four.

4. Breathe in...two, three, four. - Hold...two, three, four. - exhale...two, three, four. - Pause...two, three, four.

5. Breathe in...two, three, four. - Hold...two, three, four. - exhale...two, three, four. - Pause...two, three, four.

6. Inhale...two, three, four. - Hold...two, three, four. - exhale...two, three, four. - Pause...two, three, four.

7. Breathe in...two, three, four. - Hold...two, three, four. - exhale...two, three, four. - Pause...two, three, four.

8. Breathe in...two, three, four. - Hold...two, three, four. - exhale...two, three, four. - Pause...two, three, four.

9. Breathe in...two, three, four. - Hold...two, three, four. - exhale...two, three, four. - Pause...two, three, four.

10. Inhale...two, three, four. - Hold...two, three, four. - exhale...two, three, four. - Pause...two, three, four.

11. Breathe in...two, three, four. - Hold...two, three, four. - exhale...two, three, four. - Pause...two, three, four.

12. Breathe in...two, three, four. - Hold...two, three, four. - exhale...two, three, four. - Pause...two, three, four.

13. Breathe in...two, three, four. - Hold...two, three, four. - exhale...two, three, four. - Pause...two, three, four.

14. Inhale...two, three, four. - Hold...two, three, four. - exhale...two, three, four. - Pause...two, three, four.

15. Breathe in...two, three, four. - Hold...two, three, four. - exhale...two, three, four. - Pause...two, three, four.

F – Emotion-Stirring Music

The main background music used in this audiobook is from mettaverse.com. They have an amazing selection of binaural beats and soundscapes. You can also check out their YouTube channel: Mettaverse Music.

As a final bonus, I've shared 12 random songs from my Spotify and YouTube playlists below. They vary from feel-good progressive instrumentals and meditation music to orchestra sounds and even some hip-hop. You won't like them all, but I think some will resonate. I could have picked 100 songs. I genuinely believe that getting a quality pair of headphones or going for a drive and playing this type of music can get you out of a rut and inspire you, no matter how good or bad your day is going.

They all stir up emotions and spark a reaction in different ways. You've probably noticed the deep intense nature of this book and the affirmations. Well, that theme continues in my music selection.

The Hans Zimmer entire playlist is genuinely breathtaking, particularly the opening part, which is the Interstellar soundtrack (watch this movie if you haven't already). And if you play the HipHop or progressive music and hit the gym treadmill, no matter how bad you feel, you will run for miles and feel great after.

The list is in no particular order, but the first half contains the instrumental type and then progresses to more modern songs. Helpful tip: if you find any specific song inspiring, hit the 'Go Radio' button of that song on Spotify, and you will find endless songs with a similar feel and vibe. That's how I find all my music. It's incredible how music can stir up different emotions inside and give you energy and inspiration from nowhere. I hope you enjoy!

1. Now We Are Free – Lisa Gerrard, Klaus Badelt, Hans Zimmer
2. The Celtic of Scotland (Original Mix) – Dinka
3. Hans Zimmer – Ultimate Soundtrack Compilation Mix (YouTube)
4. Void Lights – 36
5. Crystal Cave – Lesh, Lumidelic
6. Cambodia – Tony Anderson, Eyra Moon
7. Escape (feat. Hayla) – Kx5, deadmau5, Kaskade, Hayla
8. Fly Like an Eagle – Seal
9. FKA twigs – Two Weeks
10. Holiday – Confidence Man
11. Too Late – The Weeknd
12. Champion (feat. Chris Brown) – Chip, Chris Brown

CONCLUSION – PERSPECTIVE

To conclude this book, I want to give you a broader perspective on your life. People talk about practicing gratitude and being thankful for what you have in life. It's something that's so important, but there will be days you simply won't feel up to it. You'll feel like life is getting you down, or you're having no luck. We've all been there. It's hard to just feel grateful for no reason. It's hard to pull those emotions out of thin air. But if you really step back and take a broad view of things, you can do it.

First of all, you need to realize that your life span is just a blip in time, a drop in the ocean, compared to how long the earth and universe have been in existence. If you just happened to be born a mere 100 years earlier, another blip in time, think how different your life would be. You could be facing war or famine. You might not have food on the table. You won't have a TV, never mind the internet. You might meet a person once and then literally never see them again. The fact that you even get to be an athlete, play a sport, or compete in an event is a blessing in itself. If you go back another hundred years, most sports didn't exist, at least not in the form they are played in today.

Secondly, unfortunately, there is still war and famine happening in many countries to this day. You most likely do not live in one of those countries, and if you do, more power to you. There is a reason that poorer regions of the world often create the greatest athletes in the world. While unfortunately, most won't make it out of disadvantaged areas, those that do often go on to achieve great things. Just look at the talent Brazil produces from kids playing on the street from a young age.

The great Brazilian footballer Ronaldo (not Cristiano Ronaldo) had trials for a top local team as a teenager. Unfortunately, he could not afford the bus fare to take him to the trial and was beaten up and robbed on his way home. He went on to win two world cups and become the best player in the world at that time.

So if you do come from a less developed area, you will most likely be born into a life of obstacles. If you can make it passed those, you will already have the spirit needed to make it to the top. You just have to stay disciplined. If not, appreciate that you are lucky to have this opportunity, and take it with both hands.

It's important to put your adversity into perspective. Take a look back at all the greats in history as well as your sporting heroes of the past. Read up on Gandhi, Nelson Mandela, Rosa Parks, Roald Amundsen, and Napoleon. Take a look at what they achieved. Read up on the Roman emperors and the Greek philosophers. You'll soon find inspiration from somewhere.

Nowadays, it's very easy to get caught up in worrying about petty things. Social media has young kids and adults comparing themselves to millionaires and successful athletes every minute of the day. Next time you are worried or stressed about something small, just remember what the people before you have gone through. What your ancestors have been through. Count your blessings, and be thankful that you get to lace up your boots and take on a dream. I know it works for me, giving me true perspective and gratitude when worried or facing a difficult situation.

No matter what part of the journey of life you are on, there is always hope; there is always a comeback that can happen, a redemption. I sincerely wish you the best and hope you go after your dream in whatever field you choose. Best of luck!

<u>REFERENCES</u>

Clear, J. (2021). *Atomic habits: Tiny changes, remarkable results: An easy & proven way to build Good Habits & Break Bad Ones*. CELA.

Frankl, V. E. (2021). *Man's search for meaning*. Rider.

Goddard, N., & Allen, D. (2016). *The neville goddard collection*. Shanon Allen.

Godin, S., & Macleod, H. (n.d.). *The dip*. Portfolio.

Marcus, P. (2022). *20 Game Changers in History Series 1*. PatrickMarcusBooks.

Mettaverse Music (no date) *Mettaverse*. Available at: https://mettaverse.com/ (Accessed: November 24, 2022).

Hawkins, D. R. (2014). *Letting go: The pathway to surrender*. Hay House, Inc.

Tolle, E. (2004). *The power of now: A guide to spiritual enlightenment.* Distributed to the trade by Publishers Group West.

WebMD. (n.d.). *Box breathing: Getting started with box breathing, how to do it, benefits and tips.* WebMD. Retrieved November 2, 2022, from https://www.webmd.com/balance/what-is-box-breathing

<ahref="https://lovepik.com/images/png-athlete.html">Athlete Png vectors by Lovepik.com</a>

ABOUT AUTHOR

Brian O'Grady is a High-school Teacher and coach with numerous credentials in both his coaching and playing career. Brian has coached successful high school and local soccer and basketball teams for 10+ years. He has also been involved in elite-level sports as an athlete himself, performing at national games and championships in athletics, soccer, and basketball. Brian is also a successful businessman and entrepreneur, working as a digital marketer and freelancer. Brian has been a believer in mediation and affirmations for a long time, which helped him tremendously throughout his athletic and business careers. He has been studying sports psychology for several years and believes that mindset and being able to overcome adversity is the most crucial aspect of success.